CONTENTS

McLUHAN IN AN AGE OF SOCIAL MEDIA

Paul Levinson

ISBN 978-1-56178-050-1
Photograph on book cover by Paul Levinson
Published by Connected Editions

INTRODUCTION

It's been more than two decades since I wrote *Digital McLuhan: A Guide to the Information Millennium*, published in 1999. This essay may be considered a new chapter in that book.

The digital world today is very different than the way it was then, when there was no Facebook, Twitter, or YouTube, no smart-phones or tablets, in short, no social media and the devices we carry in our pockets to be in touch with these media 24 hours a day. And yet, Marshall McLuhan's ideas, which described so well the early days of the Internet in the 1990s, have even greater applicability to the media of today, which turns all of us into producers, able to create and disseminate a text, photograph, or video as easily as we can receive them. McLuhan's notion of the "global village," little more than a brilliant metaphor when McLuhan wrote about it in *The Gutenberg Galaxy* in 1962 – when the newest medium in town, television, was national not global, with a one-way non-interactive audience unlike the bustling village – is even more at hand as the 21st century progresses, demonstrating itself in everything from politics and the Arab Spring to literally global musical performances such as Playing for Change (Eller, 2016). Although singing has yet to become globally telepathic as in the 2016 *Sense8* Christmas special, it and many other kinds of communication are well on the way.

I therefore thought it might be a good time to offer this brief update of *Digital McLuhan*, a chapter that would fit well into that book it were published today, in which I now detailed how McLuhan's poetic, controversial, but uniquely useful concepts can help us make sense of the world in which live, of the media that surround us and we rely upon, and which are evolving so rapidly as to make any printed essay or chapter about them likely obsolete the day it was published. But one of the advantages of our digital age, and of publications such as this one on Amazon, is that they can be updated at any time, which is what I promise to do with this essay, as new apps and patterns of media usage emerge.

Let us begin with McLuhan's tetrad, and what it can tell us about the selfie.

TETRADS OF VISION AND SNAPCHAT

The tetrad, in a nutshell, is a way of mapping the impact and interconnections of technologies across time. It asks four questions of every medium or technology: What does it enhance or amplify? What does it obsolesce or push out of the sunlight and into the shade? What does it retrieve or bring back into central attention and focus – something which itself had been previously obsolesced. And what does the new medium, when pushed to its limits, reverse or flip into?

As an example, the photograph amplifies literal visual memory, capturing the world as it actually is. The photograph obsolesces painting, drawing, and sketching, which rely on the painter's interpretation as much or more than the subject of the painting. The photograph retrieves the reflection of the world in a pool of water, which also shows the world as it really is. And the photograph flips into motion photography, three-dimensional holography, and, most recently, into the instant and immediately universally transferable digital image.

The multiplicity of pieces in that fourth part of the tetrad – motion photography, holography, digital photography – applies to all parts of the four-part probe. The photograph also obsolesces verbal and written descriptions of events – hence, a photograph can be worth even more than a thousand words – and the photograph also retrieves photographic memory. But the flip provides the entrée to the future, so let's unpack it a little more regarding that photographic flip into the digital image.

The selfie would be a prime example of one of the social media the photograph has flipped into. I realized this after posting on Twitter a photograph of Marshall McLuhan, Eric McLuhan and me taken at the "Tetrad Conference" I organized at Fairleigh Dickinson University in 1978. Media theorist Ian Bogost, tweeting about the photograph, asked me "where's the fourth"? I immediately tweeted in reply – the fourth is the selfie – by which I meant, the fourth figure in that photograph, not yet emerged in 1978, was no one other than the threesome already in the photograph, any one of whom could have taken the photograph as a selfie in 2014. In the selfie, the camera in the phone literally flips around from pointing at the outside world to pointing at the face of the photographer.

Paul Levinson, Marshall McLuhan, Eric McLuhan, 1978

As is the case with all tetrads, we can do a four-part mapping of the flipped medium. Thus, the selfie amplifies the merging of photographer and subject, obsolesces the world as our tableau, retrieves looking at our own reflection in the pool of water or the mirror, and flips into ... well, how about Snapchat, which invites dissemination of images, including selfies, that disappear seconds or minutes after posting?

Snapchat, indeed, as well as "stories" on Instagram and Facebook, can also be seen as media that the photograph itself flips into, when we trace the photograph as a medium of permanence, or, extension across time. André Bazin (1962/1967), the film critic, hit upon this effect of photography perfectly, when he observed that the photograph rescues an image from its "proper corruption in time". In that track, the photograph obsolesces fleeting images and memories, retrieves images carved into stone, and now reverses, in the digital age, back to the ephemeral immediacy of Snapchat.

And Snapchat reverses another important aspect not only of traditional photography but digital photographic apps such as Pinterest: Snapchat, like Twitter, is an immediate and impulsive medium. In the first years of its existence in the 1840s, the very taking of the photograph took long minutes, which is why the human subjects of those photographs are not smiling. The speed in which the photograph could be seen by the nonprofessional photographer remained slow, dependent upon the mail system or when a photography shop was open, until the Polaroid camera debuted a full century later. And even in our age of social media, people take much more time and care when posting photos to Pinterest and Instagram than they do for Snapchat. (A student in one of my classes told me she and her friends often look over and debate whether to put a photo of themselves on Instagram, whether to apply this or that filter, or perhaps a "Facetune" app, in contrast to posting a photo almost on whim on Snapchat.) This stems from the evanescence of Snapchat photographs – there's less at stake for your reputation if the image will be gone in 24 hours. Mapping this out in a tetrad, we could say that Snapchat amplifies casual abandon in photography, obsolesces the careful attention accorded to Instagram postings, retrieves the textual speed of Twitter, and reverses into ... well, since December 2012, Snapchat offers the option of video, recapitulating the reversal of photography (and radio) into television in the 1920s (when television was invented) and the 1940s (when television became a mass medium).

Snapchat is also an excellent, less metaphoric example of what Tony Schwartz (1973) had in mind when he observed that television treats the eye "like an ear". McLuhan had earlier noted in *The Gutenberg Galaxy* (1962) that civilization had swapped our ears for eyes, a momentous step in what he saw as an artificial division of the senses, which put the visual mode in the driver's seat, and engendered literacy and the Renaissance among other things. Television restored some of the lost acoustic to the visual by introducing a key acoustic property – a message everywhere at once – in its mass, simultaneous broadcasts. TV was evanescent as well, another acoustic characteristic, but this was seen as a limitation of a nascent medium, and was soon corrected by video tape recorders, DVDs, video on demand, and, most recently, streaming. Snapchat, in contrast, was deliberately designed to be fleeting from the outset. It thus can be considered an intentionally acoustic visual medium. We might call it an acoustic photograph.

Moreover, the instantaneity and fleeting quality of Snapchat postings make it an ideal vehicle for the conveyance of breaking news, with links to the fuller stories, which it is increasingly becoming (WashPostPR, 2017). As historical context, the first time I ever encountered a major news story online before anyplace else was in 1997 about the death of Princess Diana (Levinson, 1999, p. 7) and the last time I was informed of breaking news for the first time in a newspaper was in 1978, about the death of former Israeli Prime Minister Golda Meir, which I learned about by glancing at a late edition of the *New York Daily News* on a now bygone newsstand in downtown Manhattan. We could do a tetrad of this aspect of Snapchat as follows: amplifies immediately breaking news with a speed that depends only on posting a photo and a headline, with links to the story elsewhere on the Web; obsolesces every place else on the Web as a source of breaking news; retrieves the town crier, and the instantaneous, immediately vanishing nature of the human voice, and reverse into ... still too soon to fully tell, but video will no doubt be a part of it.

We can further employ the tetrad to put into context other visual components of the social media revolution. Google Glass, for example, fit quite well into the fourth part of a tetrad about eyeglasses, which enhance clearer vision, obsolesce poor eyesight, retrieve the keen naked vision we may have had when we were younger, and flip into Google Glass which lets us see anything, anytime, anywhere in the world, online. Although Google Glass failed to attract much continuing public interest, it pointed the way to "wearable" media, and the Apple smart watch, which does much the same as far as extending our vision as Google Glass. We could do a separate tetrad for the Apple Watch, in which the traditional watch, which tells us the time, flips into the Apple Watch, which allows us to see *through* time – or, at least, to the past, when we use the Apple Watch to see the past on the Internet. Snapchat Spectacles – sunglasses which take videos instantly transmissible to Snapchat – is in effect a more limited version of Google Glass, easier to use, and has constituted "a craze" (Harding, 2016).

Photography in the age of social media provides another tableau amenable to an explication via the tetrad. At the Book Salon at the McLuhan Centre in the Coach House at the University of Toronto on January 27, 2016 for this very essay, *McLuhan in an Age of Social Media*, Ira Nayman observed that the global village has flipped into the global dining room. He was referring to the ubiquity of the smartphone at dinner tables at home and in restaurants, but another even more vivid expression of this reversal of the global village into the global dining room instantly occurred to me: the omnipresent photographs of food, what people are about to eat, on tables before them, taken on smartphones and uploaded to Instagram, Facebook, and Pinterest, has literally turned the table on the global village, making it a world smorgasbord or global dining room, a constellation of images of what all us are eating.

Left to right: Hugh Spencer, Paul Levinson, and Ira Nayman at the Book Salon at the McLuhan Centre Coach House, January 27, 2016. (For a summary via tweets of some of the salient points discussed at this Book Salon, see Kornfeld, 2016.)

Meanwhile, the smartphone itself is in the process of undergoing a tetradic flip. It burst onto the scene in 2007 as a ubiquitously portable means of access to everything on the Internet, which I had earlier termed the "medium of media" (Levinson, 1999, p. 5). By 2018, some eleven years later, the smartphone was already being used for everything from going to a movie to getting into your hotel room (Lawson, 2018). In other words, the smartphone had begun to flip from a universal accessor of information to a magic wand that quite literally opens all kinds of tangible doors. And the speed of media evolution is such that the phone as magic wand has already begun to flip back into the human face itself, which via facial recognition can pay for meals and rides in the next generation of amusement parks (Brzeski, 2019).

The tetrad of course can also put into clearer context not only the process of seeing and the images we may see, and the vehicles through which we see them, but something else that we do with our eyes: reading. This invites a discussion of what McLuhan might have said about the Kindle – a topic so important that it deserves a section of its own.

THE KINDLE: ELEGY FOR THE PAPERBACK WRITER

The book's flip into the Kindle not only replaces paper with screens, print with pixels, but has spearheaded a profound revolution in the gatekeeping of media which was the hallmark of media dissemination prior to the digital age.

I was always struck by the loss to humanity of what Thomas Gray described in his "Elegy in a Country Churchyard" (1751) poem – a paean to all the "mute inglorious Miltons" who are buried without anyone ever knowing of their great work, because fortune declined to shine on them.

And fortune usually came in the form of gatekeepers, who decided what would be printed and what would not. Occasionally, we would get a glimpse of what the gatekeepers – acquisition editors and publishers – had kept out, people like John Kennedy Toole, whose novel *A Confederacy of Dunces* (1980) won the Pulitzer Prize for Fiction a year after it was published, unfortunately eleven years after the author, despondent about being turned down by the traditional press, took his own life.

By the time I wrote *Digital McLuhan* at the end of the 20th century, some of the gates were already creaking a bit open. But the advent of social media in the first decade of the 21st century flung them asunder, far and wide. Bloggers for the first time were able to publish their thoughts on whatever topic without anyone's permission. Then Facebook and Twitter allowed instant, global commentary on any subject.

The Kindle and what it did for the book was the icing on this cake. McLuhan himself was not immune to the destructive gatekeeping of traditional publishing. I remember well when he came to New York from Toronto, for the Tetrad Conference I mentioned earlier, with a box of "remaindered" copies of *Take Today: The Executive as Dropout* (1972) – remaindered, or taken off the market and given to the author for a dollar per book, because the publisher had determined that the book was not selling well enough to warrant its continued publication.

What Amazon has done for the book with its Kindle is allow any author, any human being, McLuhan or a complete unknown, to publish books. I have benefitted from this myself as an author. My science fiction novels began to be offered as Kindle editions in 2012 – having previously been published in hardcover and paperback by a big traditional publisher – and my novels have sold more books as Kindles since then than any time after they were first brought out years before by my traditional publisher. Other advantages of Kindle in contrast to traditional publishing of books for authors include the ability to publish a book hours after it has been completed (in comparison to the many months or years required in traditional publishing) and make edits in the book any time after it has been published. The very book that you are now reading, for example, has been updated more than thirty times since it first was published in October, 2015. The most recent update is two-fold: (a) my mention in the previous section of the smartphone flipping into the face as a medium of purchase, and (b) consequently the previous words in this sentence (part a, which of course changes every time this book is updated). I added them both on October 17, 2019.

An additional series of advantages to authors of Kindle books pertain to sales, beginning with their being visible to the author/ publisher immediately and royalties payable monthly (in comparison to once or at best twice a year in traditional publishing). Indeed, in the case of ebooks "borrowed" via the Kindle Unlimited program, authors are paid per pages read, and receive reports of the number of pages read in a book almost in real time. There was nothing even remotely possible like this for authors of paperback and hardcover books, unless you were willing to spend days in a library or bookstore, in the hope that someone would take your novel off the shelf, and read it right there in front of your very eyes. Further, authors in the United States and most countries receive no payment for books borrowed from libraries, in contrast to a small but better-than-nothing payment (a fraction of a cent) from Amazon for each page read in a Kindle borrow. And for books sold rather than borrowed, royalties are usually 70% of the list price of the book, in comparison to the 10% authors regularly received for sales of their books from traditional publishers.

Readers also benefit from this immediacy, which allows the book to have a topicality previously attainable in print only in the age of newspapers and their multiple editions during the day. McLuhan in *Understanding Media* (1964) had already cited with agreement French poet Alphonse de Lamartine's circa 1830 lamentation that "the book arrives too late." A decade later, McLuhan also noted "the Xerox makes everyone a publisher" (1977). I entitled my 2014 article about McLuhan in the *Journal of Visual Culture* "The Kindle Arrives in Time and Makes Everyone a Publisher" to underline the role of the Kindle in this evolution of the book. In terms of the tetrad, the Kindle retrieves – in addition to authorial control – the immediacy of classic, multiple-edition newspapers. (As for the flip, the Kindle is still too new for a fourth part of that tetrad to be clearly seen.)

But the Kindle has already had another impact in its partial obsolescence of the printed volume. One of McLuhan's most useful observations has been his discovery that new technologies transform older devices into art forms. In McLuhan's time, motion pictures had already pushed theater, once a medium of the masses, onto the "legitimate," i.e., culturally and intrinsically worthy, stage. The typewriter had turned good penmanship from a necessity into an admirable talent. And writing itself had for millennia made poetry, needed as a mnemonic in Homer's time, into a high form of culture. In *Digital McLuhan*, I added my own examples. Delicatessen, once spiced with natural and artificial preservatives as a way of preserving the meat, became in an age of refrigeration something to be prized for its taste. And speaking of cooling, people once drove around in convertible cars to keep physically cool – until air conditioning did that more reliably, which led to people driving convertibles to look, i.e., be culturally, cool.

In December 2015 the *Guardian* published an article about a bookstore in Japan which stocked and displayed just one book at a time (Flood, 2015). The emporium had just opened in May 2015. In the age of the Kindle, the physical book, whatever may be on its pages, is a worthy candidate for singular exhibition, just as the Japanese are wont to do by placing a single painting to be admired without competition on a wall. (For a deft analysis of the recent evolution, current status, and very likely future of the retail bookstore by a once Barnes & Noble employee and now Amazon best-selling author, see Howey, 2016.)

THE ARAB SPRING

As the article about the bookstore in *The Guardian* suggests, newspapers as well as books continue to play important roles in multiple forms, digital and physical, in the age of social media. Newspapers in particular have always brought the political consequences of media into sharper focus. McLuhan was at his most daring and provocative when he gauged the political impact of media, noting in *Understanding Media* (1964, p. 261), for example, that with no radio, we would not have had an Adolf Hitler, given that Hitler's rhetoric didn't withstand the logical scrutiny of print, and Hitler looked nothing like the Aryan ideal he preached, and thus would have been self-refuting on television. There have been equally archetypal examples of McLuhan's "medium is the message" in the 21st century.

In *New New Media* (2nd edition, 2013), I examined the question of whether social media were a necessary condition for the Arab Spring. The qualification of "necessary" in contrast to "sufficient" as an adjective of "condition" is crucial here. Just as the elevator was a necessary but not sufficient condition for skyscrapers – which also required a technology for construction of tall buildings – so did the Arab Spring require much more than the new access to Twitter, YouTube, and media in the hands of people not governments. But the necessity of social media especially in the early waves of the Arab Spring in Tunisia and Egypt was remarked upon extensively at the time – for example, by Wael Ghonim in Egypt, who famously told CNN that "this revolution started online . . . this revolution started on Facebook" (see Evangelista, 2011, and also Levinson, 2011, for more).

The lack of total success of the Arab Spring in no way negates the role of new new media in facilitating the replacement of governments in the first place. Although revolutions may be triggered and fomented by whatever factors, including media, their long-range success usually depends on whether real improvements result in the lives of citizens, and this goes well beyond communication of grievances in the initial phases of the revolution. Thus, the instability in Egypt after the departure of Hosni Mubarak shows the limitations of social media not as facilitators of social change but as means of better governance. The same may well apply to the impact of social media on elections in contrast to what happens after elections in democratic societies.

PERISCOPE TO THE RESCUE

A notable example of the power of social media in democratic societies occurred on June 22, 2016, when House of Representative Democrats in the United States began a "sit-in" to get intransigent Republicans to consider new gun control legislation in the wake of the Orlando, Florida murder of 49 people a week earlier. The Republicans controlled the House, and with it the ability of CSPAN television to carry House events live to the nation and world. Unsurprisingly, Republican leaders of the House refused to let CSPAN do its job, and cut off its cameras.

But the United States and the world saw what was going on just fine, thanks to CSPAN picking up the video feeds on Periscope (see Kastrenakes, 2016), a free app widely available on smartphones. Unregulated by any authority other than the conscience of people who pointed their smartphones in the right direction, social media brought people the truth when political authorities thought it would be better to suppress it. When elected representatives did the wrong thing, social media allowed the people to correct that.

Unsurprisingly, the Republican-controlled Congress never did enact or even consider gun control legislation in 2016, but the point for its need was nonetheless made. And by the end of the year, Republicans indicated their concerns about Periscope – not guns – by proposing House of Representative rules that would fine any unauthorized broadcast or streaming of audio, video, or even photographs from the House floor (Bailey, 2016). Aside from this being a likely violation of the First Amendment: if history is any lesson, the totalitarian impulse is no match for ideas conveyed by innovations in communication technology, which always win in the end (see Dumbach & Newborn, 1986, for the heroic story of The White Rose resistance in Nazi Germany, mounted via primitive photocopying devices).

MCLUHAN AS TWEETER

Twitter figures not only as a medium that "softly determined" the Arab Spring – soft being a necessary condition, hard being a sufficient condition – but also as a template not just for what McLuhan wrote, but how he wrote it. Indeed, Twitter as a medium captures one of the media forms that McLuhan employed in one of his best known and most important books: the "glosses" or chapter titles in *The Gutenberg Galaxy* (1962).

Among my favorite of those 107 glosses are "Schizophrenia may be a necessary consequence of literacy" and "The new electronic interdependence recreates the world in the image of a global village." They epitomize the ideal of Twitter and its 140-character limit, in which brevity strives to be the soul of wit. Except, in McLuhan's case, the glosses conveyed not only wit but wisdom – intense, compact, far-reaching, and predictive.

As I noted throughout *Digital McLuhan*, McLuhan foresaw the digital age not because he was clairvoyant, but because his mind was in tune with the human needs for communication that the digital age now accommodates and satisfies. But the advent of social media – new new media – shows something more:

McLuhan's mode of communication was an attempt to break through the regimented strictures of traditional print media – strictures which not only got in the way of talented authors getting published, but obliged authors who were published to write in a certain way, with short chapter titles and long chapters. *The Gutenberg Galaxy* shattered both of those structures and strictures, and the advent of forms such as now seen on Twitter show that McLuhan's modes of expression were not odd or merely provocative but fundamentally human.

HILLARY CLINTON AND DONALD TRUMP PLAYED IT COOL

One of McLuhan's most celebrated – and oft-criticized and misunderstood – tools for understanding media was his distinction between "hot" versus "cool" modes of communication. A hot medium is high-profile, intense, and provides the consumer with lots of information. In contract, a cool medium is low-profile, soft, blurry, and gives the consumer much less. McLuhan's surprising insight was that the cool medium invites much more consumer participation, as the viewer, reader, or listener gets pulled in to complete the gaps. Good examples would be poetry (cool) which can occasion much more thought and discussion that a work of prose (hot) of the same length, or a cartoon drawing (cool) which can invite much more careful scrutiny that a clear photograph (hot).

McLuhan usefully applied this distinction to politics and media, famously observing that John F. Kennedy bested Richard Nixon in their 1960 television debates because Kennedy was better suited to the cool medium of television. And this kind of analysis works just as well for political events in 2015-2016.

In April 2015, Hillary Clinton released a video on YouTube – not television – in which she announced her entry into the 2016 U.S. Presidential race. Many commentators were surprised that the candidate didn't herself appear in the video until it was two-thirds finished – candidates usually appear at the beginning and very prominently throughout their video advertisements and announcements. But McLuhan's hot and cool distinction explains why: Hillary Clinton was making a low-profile, cool pitch, inviting the viewers to fill in the video with what they might most want to hear from the candidate. This was preferable to Clinton, whose positions are already well known, simply repeating them in the video.

Gail Sheehy reported in her 1999 biography, *Hillary's Choice*, that Clinton had read McLuhan and his student Walter Ong during her undergraduate studies at Wellesley College, prior to the 1968 Democratic National Convention (see Lance Strate, 2004, for details). Though the title of Clinton's famous 1996 book, *It Takes A Village*, is attributed to a variety of African proverbs that in one way or another say "It takes a village to raise a child" (see Proverb, 1996), it may not be a coincidence that Clinton came of age when McLuhan's "global village" was first achieving iconic status in the 1960s.

Bernie Sanders' hammering against the "one-percent" aka billionaires who control the American economy is a classic example of "hot" in the McLuhanesque sense, which suggests why Bernie was unlikely to win the Democratic nomination for President in 2016 in this continuingly "cool" age of ours, despite his strong initial showing. On the other hand, if he had against great odds secured the nomination, that could have been explained as our world not being as cool as it was, for example, in 1960. Or a Sanders win in our cool social environment could have been attributed to "feeling the Bern" having some cool characteristics, after all, in the lack of detailed plans in Sanders' big ideas for his "revolution," and in the non-pragmatic, almost inchoate, "revolutionary" yearning of his followers. And this "cool Bern," in turn, points to a continuing weakness and strength in McLuhan's formulations: their capacity to explain almost everything. In that sense, a hot-and-cool analysis of any phenomenon is in itself cool. But Bernie Sanders in fact did not win the Democratic Party primaries, which lends support to the classic hot-and-cool analysis without bending it into pretzel contortions.

Meanwhile, Donald Trump's use of Twitter beginning in the Summer of 2015 to attack his competitors in the 2016 Republican Presidential race as well as his critics in the media would be an especially striking example of the success of "cool" in politics, and helps explain why someone who never held political office led in the national Republican primary polls since shortly after his entry into the race in June 2015, and became the Republican nominee for President in July 2016. Although the explicitness of text might make a tweet quintessentially hot, and the scathing harshness of Trump's text especially so, its situation in the environment of Twitter, with its limit of 140 characters, makes the tweet intrinsically sketchy and cool, and accords well with the surge of sarcastic insult and lack of political depth in Trump's tweets. The inherently interactive nature of Twitter further cools these messages, which practically beg for some kind of response. (See Levinson, 1976, and Levinson, 1999, for more on the electronic cooling of hot textual media; and my quotes in Slater, 2007, for a pre-political assessment of Trump.)

Media commentator Howard Fineman (2016) described Trump's modus operandi as watching television with a smart phone in hand and tweeting his visceral reactions – or what we could characterize as immersion in two cool media – which Trump thinks connects him to the American people. His stiff performance when reading from teleprompters – for example, in his speech on June 7, 2016, right before Hillary Clinton won the California primary, denounced as "boring" by many in the media (e.g., Friedersdorf, 2016) – is further indication of his "coolness," in this case, his discomfort with the hot, literal medium of teleprompters.

The lack of specificity in Trump's positions invites people to fill in what they want to hear, and is additional evidence of his "coolness". This is why Trump was perceived at the end of August 2016 as both "softening" and "hardening" his position on immigration, and in fact proclaimed over just a few days that he was doing both (CBS News, 2016) – his position was almost completely in the eye (or ear) of the beholder, i.e., an exemplar of cool. Indeed, the almost complete lack of content in Trump's ideas and arguments – saying about foreign affairs, for example, that he gets his knowledge from what he sees on television (see Corasaniti, 2015) – makes Trump an example of what McLuhan might have a called a politician who is all medium and no content.

The violence that erupted at Trump rallies in February and March 2016 is the ultimate expression of this "cool" – the "flip," in terms of the tetrad – and another way in which the media and political environment of 2016 in the United States is similar to what transpired here in the 1960s. The clashes at Donald Trump's rally in Chicago on March 11, 2016 were disturbingly reminiscent of the violence at the Democratic National Convention in Chicago in the summer of 1968. Significantly, the cool 1960s happened a decade after the introduction of television cooled down the predominantly hot media of radio and motion pictures of the prior era, just as social media in 2015-2016 worked their cooling effect on politics a decade after Twitter and Facebook had begun to replace hot newspapers as the main written medium in politics.

The consequences of coolness, in other words, can cut both ways, leading to a "cool" politician, John F. Kennedy, becoming a much-admired President in the early 1960s, but reversing into violence internationally and domestically a little later in the same decade. Similarly, being cool can be both a blessing and a curse for any particular candidate. In addition to his awkwardness with the teleprompter, Trump's poor performance in his first debate with Clinton was generally attributed to his lack of preparation

(Healy, Parker, and Haberman, 2016), or a signal characteristic of cool. And his vulnerability to release of a recording of explicit, sexually abusive remarks in October 2016 - which caused him to plummet in the polls (Silver, 2016) and lose the support of dozens of officeholders in his own party (Easley, 2016) - speaks to the fragility of cool. We could say that cool, which taketh and well as giveth, exacted its revenge on Trump in that first debate and after (see Levinson, 2016d, for more).

At the same time, the propensity of Trump's core supporters, i.e., those most caught up in the cool, continued to see and hear whatever they most wanted in their candidate, and provided the candidate with a rock-solid foundation of devotees, whatever he actually did or said, or whatever recordings of earlier misconduct revealed. This cool foundation proved sufficient for Trump to win the Presidency in November 2016. In the end, playing it cool paid off for both candidates, albeit in different ways. Clinton won the popular vote but Trump won the electoral vote and therein the U.S. Presidency. In the aftermath of the election, Trump continued to demonstrate the coolness and lack of content in his positions, proclaiming, contrary to his numerous assertions made during the campaign, that he would not further investigate Hillary Clinton for her alleged e-mail misuse (*MorningJoe*, 2016).

In addition to cool media flipping into hot in-person violence, McLuhan also wrote about a related consequence of the television screen, noting how the steady diet of untouchable images made us "discarnate," and imbued viewers with an irresistible impulse to "reach out and touch someone" – tag-line of AT&T's advertising for the telephone at the end of the 1970s, inspired by McLuhan's (1964, p. 67) identification of "getting in touch" and "keeping in touch" as tactile metaphors for the goal of electronic acoustic communication. The actual touching could be violent – as it was in the 1960s and at Trump rallies and the world-at-large in 2015-2016 – or amorous (the connection between television and the sexual revolution) or just getting beyond the screen and into the world outside, as suddenly occurred for tens of millions of people with Pokémon Go in the summer of 2016. (See McLuhan, 1978, for more on "discarnate man"; Levinson, 1999, pp. 57-58, for more on cool media and their eliciting of real-world violence and sex; Levinson, 2003, for the symbiotic relationship of virtual and physical reality; and Sturt & Nordstrom, 2016, for the Pokémon Go phenomenon.)

It may have seemed strange to find two candidates with such differing positions on the same side of this hot and cool distinction, and both connected via McLuhan's probe of cool media to Pokémon Go, but Hillary Clinton said she's "not a natural politician" (Gass, 2016), Donald Trump (2015) said the same, and one of the advantages of McLuhan's approach always has been that it uncovers connections in unexpected places. Indeed, Clinton told a campaign rally on 14 July 2016, "I don't know who created Pokémon Go, but I've tried to figure out how we get them to have Pokémon go to the polls" (Andrews, 2016).

But the inclusion of two such different political presentations under the same cool banner nonetheless shows that "cool" is comprised of more than one ingredient, and can be better understood as a composite attained in non-identical ways. In the 1960 path-breaking television debate, both Nixon and JFK were low-key or cool in their delivery, but Nixon projected an underlying uneasy intensity in contrast to JFK, who evinced an underlying calm and being on top of it. The net result was Nixon was hot and Kennedy cool - which made JFK more suitable to television back then. In 2015-2016, Trump's outer crust was hot and abrasive, but the specifics of his hyperbole and innuendo were all but nonexistent, and made him a quintessentially cool Twitter candidate.

TRUMP AND TWITTER

Donald Trump, of course, was not only very different from Hillary Clinton in the 2016 Presidential campaign, but he is markedly different in style from any other President or candidate for President in the now bygone television age. We should not be surprised, therefore, that his brand of cool, suited to and molded by Twitter, is very different from the cool of politicians who successfully utilized television in the past.

Not only JFK, but Ronald Reagan, Bill Clinton, and even Barack Obama were each in their own ways masters of television cool. Telegenic, relaxed, usually low-to-middle key, projecting a sense of being charge without being strident, were all parts of the appeal of these previous American presidents. Obama and his campaigns were certainly no strangers to social media (see Levinson, 2009/2013 for extensive analysis of how this gave Obama an advantage, especially in the 2008 campaign), but Obama looked and sounded cool and great on television, even to the point of singing "Amazing Grace" at the funeral of South Carolina State Senator Clementa Pinckney, slain in the Charleston church shooting in 2015 (Kaufman, 2015). If poetry is cool in comparison to hot prose, then surely singing is cool in comparison to speaking.

In contrast, Trump neither sings in public nor speaks softly. His harsh, aggressive manner is glaringly inconsistent with the cool television politician. It is compatible with and indeed is a hallmark of a type of television entertainer, a carnival barker saying "you're fired," which is where Trump achieved his first pop-cultural success. But unlike some analysts (e.g., Postman, 2017), who see Trump as a triumph of the televised entertainer, and a confirmation of the public's taste for entertainment over facts and rational self-interest, I see Trump's success as a diminution and vanquishing of television itself and its characteristics in favor of a very different medium with a very different kind of cool. Trump shed television like a worn skin, and went for the very different screen of Twitter.

On Twitter, unlike television, the written word is paramount. But the words on Twitter have little in common with the hot words of print or the hot chyrons on television. However scorching the meaning of Trump's 140-character Tweets, their presentation is cool, a form of poetry, which affords readers the opportunity to invest each word with the truth they desire, much as written poetry has done for millennia.

When Trump tweets that his immigration ban "is about keeping bad people (with bad intentions) out of country" (Savranksy, 2017), his supporters don't care whether terror attacks in America were in fact conducted by people from any of the countries on Trump's ban list. They don't care about facts. They know and understand exactly what Trump means by "bad," because it is exactly what they, Trump's Twitter followers, literal and political, already know to be true. Such are the dynamics of Twitter cool.

Whether Trump is aware of any of the above is not clear. He says he prizes Twitter because it allows him to communicate directly with the American people, without his words being distorted and misreported by the "dishonest" press (Phippen, 2017). In this, Trump has something profoundly in common with Adolf Hitler, who similarly preferred hot radio because it permitted him to address the German people directly, without the mediation of a critical press (see Hitler, 1924/1971, for more).

To McLuhan's observation in *Understanding Media* that without radio we would not have had Hitler, we can now add that without Twitter we would not have Trump as President.

Indeed, Evan Williams, the co-founder of Twitter, conditionally apologized in May 2017 for the role his app may have played in the election of Donald Trump, noting that, "If it's true that he wouldn't be president if it weren't for Twitter, then yeah, I'm sorry" (Streitfeld, 2017). But are media, which like knives can be used for good (to cut our food) or bad (to cut people – bad unless the cutter is a surgeon) to be blamed for the triumph of a dangerous political candidate, or anyone with whom we may disagree? (See my "Guns, Knives, and Pillows," in Levinson, 1996b, for the inherent ethics of technology residing not in the technology but in the hands of the content creator.)

Further, a given technology can work for the benefit or detriment of the individual who is wielding it. Twitter may have helped elect Trump, but a Tweet from him during the testimony of former Ambassador to Ukraine Marie Yovanovitch at a House Intelligence Committee impeachment hearing on November 15, 2019 raised questions among members of that committee about whether that Tweet from Trump – "Everywhere Marie Yovanovitch went turned bad. She started off in Somalia, how did that go?" – might be a kind of witness intimidation and itself constitute an impeachable offense (Dugyala, 2019). Although Yovanich would likely have not known about the Tweet during her testimony had Committee Chair Adam Schiff (a Democrat) not read it to her, it certainly is not unreasonable to think that future witnesses, not wishing to be publicly and falsely lambasted by the President, might be wary about testifying and incurring the President's wrath expressed to millions in Tweets. (The problems in Somalia predated Yovanovitch's time there.)

Yet Trump for his part not only values his following on Twitter, but like all leaders with a totalitarian bent, intolerant of criticism, has sought to keep his Twitter forum pure and shield himself from some of his prominent critics including author Stephen King by blocking their Twitter accounts – an action which brought on a First Amendment lawsuit on the grounds that no President has a right to prevent citizens from seeing his public statements (Savage, 2017), a lawsuit which Trump lost (Levinson, 2019).

Radio, of course, was also favored and effectively employed not only by Hitler but by democratic leaders such as FDR and Churchill (see Levinson, 1997, "Radio Heads," pp. 86-90, for details), who didn't have an animus toward professional reporters and exulted in the interplay of established media and the democratic process, so the example of Hitler and radio does not mean radio is inherently evil or totalitarian, and the same can be said of Trump and Twitter.

Much was made of Trump's firing his first Secretary of State, Rex Tillerson, in March 2018 via Twitter (McDermott, 2018). The action not the firing was seen as demeaning because the medium Trump chose is still seen in 2018 by so many talking heads on television as trivial. But Twitter is as natural and appropriate to Trump as radio was to FDR and television to JFK. Whether by guile or inchoate instinct, Trump chose Twitter as his medium during the 2016 campaign, and continues to use it as President, because he understands its advantages over television, radio, and the press: he can reach his people 24-hours-a-day, without intermediaries, wherever they and he might happen to be. Any Democrat in the 2020 election will have a hard time beating Trump in the Electoral College unless that candidate uses Twitter or an equivalent social medium as effectively as does Trump.

In the future, we can expect leaders perhaps even more adept at Twitter than is Trump. Bypassing the press, having direct access to the people, will always be irresistible to politicians of all stripes – in democracies, dictatorships, and democracies on their way to dictatorships.

FAKE NEWS, NEWS BUBBLES, AND NARCISSUS NARCOSIS

The decline of television and increasing reliance on Twitter as the go-to political medium also encouraged the advent of "fake news" – itself facilitated by the cool tendency of people to see and hear what they most want to encounter in news reports – which arguably helped turn the election in Trump's favor, with such flagrant examples as: the Pope endorsed Trump, and, an FBI agent investigating Hillary's emails was found murdered (see Davis, 2016, and Van Susteren, 2016, for more). Indeed, the very concept of fake news is so malleable and cool-gone-wild that it is now used by Trump who won the election as an epithet for any news organization which uncritically (in his view) reports on an allegedly fake news story published elsewhere (for example, in his 11 January 2017 press conference, where he denounced CNN's Senior White House correspondent as "you're fake news!"; see video, CNN, 2017).

Fake news is also supported by "news bubbles," in turn made possible by what McLuhan (1964, p. 15) called "narcissus narcosis," a fundamental aspect of media life complementary or analogous to cool, in which people seek out, find refuge in, and are most comfortable with their own reflections in media presentations (see Levinson, 2016e, for more on news bubbles, and Levinson 2016f and 2016g for comparison of fake news to government propaganda, professional journalism, and citizen journalism). Certainly the selfie would be a ubiquitous example of people in the past few years prizing their own reflections, literally.

Other than a post I put on my blog (Levinson, 2015a) right after I first saw the Clinton video, few commentators have brought McLuhan into assessments of these important political events. Lawrence O'Donnell did cite *Understanding Media* and "hot and cool" in his apt analysis on MSNBC on 22 October 2015 of Hillary Clinton's Congressional testimony about Benghazi, as did Pulitzer Prize-winning journalist Eugene Robinson on 18 July 2016 in his explanation of why someone watching a speech in-person at the Republican National Convention might have a different reaction than someone watching the same speech on the cooler medium of television, and Arthur Hunt (2016) and Jonathan Moreno (2016) each discussed Trump as a "hot" candidate – an appraisal with which I disagree, but at least it sees the value of bringing McLuhan into the picture. The rest of the academic world continues, for the most part, to adhere to the traditions that McLuhan sought to overcome, and ignore or misrepresent his work (see Pooley, 2016, for a recent, typical exercise in sarcasm regarding McLuhan's relevance to the study of media).

As an instructive point of comparison, Wythoff, 2016, notes that Hugo Gernsback, generally regarded by the academic world as a founding parent of science fiction not a media theorist, also thought and frequently wrote about media in ways very similar to McLuhan, some 40 years prior to the Canadian thinker. I would add that this academic myopia is likely due to most media scholars having as little conversance with McLuhan as they do with Gernsback's nonfiction (see Levinson, 2017a, for more on Wythoff, Gernsback, and McLuhan).

McLuhan saw media not only as worthy of poetic study, but in dynamic, aggressive conflict, with new media always vying with older media to be leader of the pack – a process that the tetrad tries to map. I put this as media being in a kind of constant Darwinian evolution, in a survival of the fittest struggle in which we humans not nature call the winners (Levinson, 1979, 1997). In the 2016 U. S. Presidential election, Twitter toppled television as the predominant political medium, just as television did to radio in the 1950s. Using your Twitter app not only to keep abreast of breaking political developments but express your opinion about them is not only easier than getting to a place with a big screen but more satisfying, and everyone other than some of the talking heads on television knows this. Twitter has bested television as a medium for coverage of most live events, but there are holdouts – like the Byzantine Empire surviving the fall of the Roman – such as the Super Bowl and its 110+ million viewers, and the first Clinton-Trump Presidential debate, which attracted a record-breaking audience exceeding 80 million people (see Levinson, 2016c; Stelter, 2016).

Television is now also increasingly watched on smart phones, and the medium in all of its sizes and systems of delivery has also been enjoying a new golden age of drama.

"COOL" CONCLUSIONS TO TWO ICONIC TELEVISION SHOWS

One of McLuhan's signal contributions in the 1960s is that he took television seriously, worthy of scholarly study, at a time when most academics gave television the contemptuous lack of treatment we see offered today about Twitter, YouTube, and social media. McLuhan's hot and cool continues to be an excellent lens through which to see television, and brings into clearer focus the finales of two of the most important televisions shows of the 21st century, and for that matter, in all of television history.

The Sopranos concluded in June 2007 with an ending that made millions of viewers think that something had gone wrong with their cable connection: the screen went to black, without warning, at a crucial moment, leaving us in doubt and obliged to scramble for whatever clues we could find about what happened to Tony Soprano. The ambiguous ending has a long history in narratives, from the last lines of *Hamlet* ("rest is silence" – does "rest" mean remainder or death?) to those of Frank R. Stockton's "The Lady or the Tiger," and as in the black screen in *The Sopranos*, McLuhan's cool puts them into context: these lack of answers provide an irresistible invitation to readers and viewers to provide their own (see Levinson, 2007, for more).

Significantly, Hillary and Bill Clinton made an ad with a comical take on The Sopranos' ending in her 2008 Presidential campaign – another example of her affinity for "cool" in politics – but it was no match for Obama's mastery over nascent, supremely cool social media (see Levinson, 2007b, for more).

David Chase was the creator of *The Sopranos* and responsible for the ending. But Matthew Weiner wrote four episodes for the last season, and his own series, *Mad Men*, debuted just a month after *The Sopranos* concluded, in July 2007. The finale of *Mad Men* in May 2015 was also deeply ambiguous, though not as starkly black-and-white as *The Sopranos*, because *Mad Men* after was not a narrative about suburban murderers. Rather, *Mad Men* was about advertising, and it fittingly concluded with a famously successful commercial for Coca-Cola, "the real thing".

But who made it? Was it Don Draper, last seen spaced out in a hippy therapy commune in California? We don't know, is the answer – which, again, invites us as viewers to provide our own answers, which forges deeper connections to the narrative (see Levinson, 2015b).

Indeed, this ending is doubly or even trebly cool, because the commercial itself was about virtually nothing, or nothing important in the grand scheme of things, a soft drink. It was the real thing about an unreal thing, like most of advertising, generated by professionals to coax the world at large to provide their own stories about the project, take it to heart, and buy it.

Matthew Weiner is clearly conversant with McLuhan. In the sixth episode of *Mad Men*, Joan tells Peggy that "the medium is the message". The episode takes place in the summer of 1960 – four years before *Understanding Media* made that aphorism so famous, but slightly after its appearance in McLuhan's typescript report for the National Association of Educational Broadcasters, U.S.

Department of Health, Education, and Welfare in June, 1960, and two years after the phrase appeared in an article McLuhan published in the *National Association of Educational Broadcasters Journal* in October, 1958, so it's just possible that erudite Joan may have come across or heard those words somewhere (see Levinson, 2007c, for more details).

TETRAD ON BINGE WATCHING AND BINGE LISTENING

At the other end of the spectrum – at the beginning rather than the end of *The Sopranos*, in its 24th episode, aired in 2000 – a nurse in a hospital laughs when a U. S. Marshal arrives and says his name is McLuhan. The episode was written by Terence Winter and directed by Tim Van Patten, but Weiner had to be aware of it.

I recall that I binge-watched the first four seasons of the series. In those days – in early 2003 – I did this via what now seem cumbersome VHS tapes. *The Sopranos*, along with *Alias* and *24*, were among the first television shows I ever binge-watched, as the best way of catching up to current episodes in the series. I recall being a little disappointed when the binge-watching – usually a period of three or four nights per season for me – was over. I found this kind of story-telling very different from seeing episodes weekly, and invigorating. Like millions of other people, I now enthusiastically binge-watch everything from *House of Cards* to *The Man in the High Castle*, not as a way of catching up, but of uniquely enjoying a story on television.

A tetrad on binge-watching would look like this: It amplifies all-at-once, continuous, uninterrupted viewing; obsolesces episodic television and talk at the water-cooler about each episode (near the end of the Fall 2015 half season of *The Talking Dead*, host Chris Hardwick lamented the decline of talking to friends about individual episodes during the week – in our new world of binge watching, individual episodes are not usually discussed); retrieves the motion picture (the long motion picture, especially), the *Nicholas Nickleby* play (8 and ½ hours), and believe it or not, a play named *The Bald Soprano*, 23 and ½ hours in length. And binge-watching also retrieves the literary form of novels first appearing as serial chapters (as with Charles Dickens) or a series of short stories (as with Isaac Asimov's *Foundation* trilogy – see Levinson, 1996a, for more on this aspect of Asimov). We could even say that the novel caters to the same thirst as binge-watching for experiencing the complete story in a single or limited number of encounters, under the reader's (viewer's) rather than publisher's (TV network's) control, making the binge-watched television series even more of a novel on television than an actual novel adapted to television.

As to what binge-watching reverses into, the debut of *Making a Murderer* on Netflix on December 18, 2015 points to at least one new form: the 10-hour drama flips into a 10-hour documentary, fiction becomes news, with a presentation of such impact on the real world that the streaming series engendered a petition to the White House to pardon the two life-imprisoned subjects of the documentary, and the online petition quickly gained more than 100,000 signatures (see Levinson, 2016a, for more). On August 12, 2016, a Federal judge overturned the conviction of one of the two defendants, now 27-year old Brendan Dassey, on grounds that his confession (the unfair circumstances of which were vividly presented in the documentary) was "involuntary under the Fifth and Fourteen Amendments" to the U. S. Constitution (see Campbell, 2016). Fiction in television binge-watching has flipped into reality to the point of leading to the release of an illegally life-imprisoned teenager.

And, in another kind of flip, we could say that binge-watching television reverses into what I would call binge-listening to radio, which is what happens when we listen to a channel devoted to one band's music, hours and hours, day after day. What I've been doing with The Beatles Channel, which debuted on Sirius/XM Radio in May 2017 (see Hill, 2017), would be a notable example, in which the binging on television reverses into binging on its literal media predecessor, radio. I realized as soon as I heard Paul McCartney's 1973 "Let Me Roll It" on The Beatles Channel that I was ear-witness to a roll of the tetrad from binge-watching to binge-listening. The result in the case of this channel is an immersion in sixty years of music from one group and its members, which is longer than the real time in which even the longest-running television dramatic series was created.

MCLUHAN ON THE FRONT PAGE OF *THE NEW YORK TIMES*

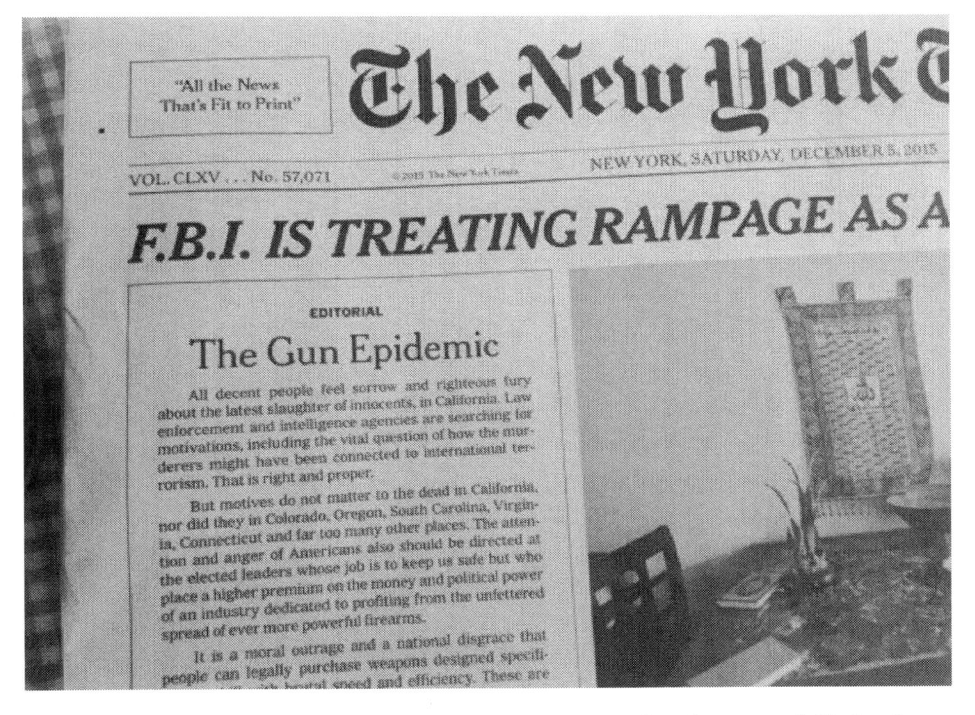

"All the News
That's Fit to Print"

The New York T

VOL. CLXV . . . No. 57,071

NEW YORK, SATURDAY, DECEMBER 5, 2015

F.B.I. IS TREATING RAMPAGE AS A

EDITORIAL

The Gun Epidemic

All decent people feel sorrow and righteous fury
about the latest slaughter of innocents, in California. Law
enforcement and intelligence agencies are searching for
motivations, including the vital question of how the murderers might have been connected to international ter-
rorism. That is right and proper.

But motives do not matter to the dead in California,
nor did they in Colorado, Oregon, South Carolina, Virgin-
ia, Connecticut and far too many other places. The attention and anger of Americans also should be directed at
the elected leaders whose job is to keep us safe but who
place a higher premium on the money and political power
of an industry dedicated to profiting from the unfettered
spread of ever more powerful firearms.

It is a moral outrage and a national disgrace that
people can legally purchase weapons designed specifi-

On December 5, 2015, *The New York Times* published an editorial on its front page, urging better gun control laws in the United States, in the aftermath of the murder of 12 people in San Bernardino earlier in the week, the latest in years of mass killings in America by people wielding guns, legally purchased and otherwise. Aside from the content of the editorial, its placement on the front page (the first such placement since 1920, when the *Times* decried the Republican nomination of Warren G. Harding for President) received enormous commentary, including in places as far away as New Zealand, where I was interviewed two mornings later on the *Breakfast* radio show about the editorial on the front page.

McLuhan pegged the importance of the front page of a newspaper more than half a century ago when he observed, in *The Mechanical Bride* in 1951, that you could get a clear sense of the world just by looking at a newspaper's front page, as if it were a picture, before you even had read any of the content. The front page in effect is a figurative landscape of what's going on, of bigger and lesser events, which can be grasped in a glance.

Much has been written, including by me, about how paper newspapers are fading away. But anything on paper still has advantages not seen on any screen, especially the little ones on our phones. Newspapers left on tables and desks can be seen by anyone who passes by. The editorial on the front page of a newspaper thus packs a uniquely irrepressible public power (see Levinson, 2015c, for more).

LABELING VS. TAGGING

I find McLuhan's way of thinking useful in explaining media just about every day. In June 2016, I was interviewed (Levinson, 2016b) about why Millennials are more averse to being labeled as such than are Baby Boomers, Generation X'ers and the like about their generations (Pew Research, 2015).

I realized that very notion of "label" is something that comes from our print culture, in which we put written or printed labels on boxes and all kinds of things, including files in a cabinet and boxes of papers. McLuhan would say that the very concept of labeling, and certainly the practice, comes from the output of the printing press, and the need to keep track of the pieces of civilization it generates.

In contrast, how do we identify posts in social media such Facebook, Instagram, etc? We tag them. And a tag is a much less defining and confining tool than is a label. Unsurprisingly, Millennials who have come of age in a world of social media and its access to information anywhere, from anyplace, any time, are more comfortable with tags than with static and stationary/stationery labels. Tags can be much more easily changed and discarded than labels.

IN AN AGE OF ALL MEDIA: "THE MEETING IS THE MESSAGE"

The applicability of McLuhan's ideas to understanding today's newspapers and cable television and the Millennial discomfort with labels brings home what may be the most important lesson in assessing his continuing relevance to the study of the media: printed newspapers and cable are not the Internet, nor are they and the Internet social media – though social media live on the Internet, and newspapers and cable increasingly do so – but McLuhan's thinking continues to illuminate and elucidate what they do to and for us. And that is because McLuhan in his thinking and mode of expression was in touch with something which transcends the traditional culture of publishing, academe, and political and critical analysis, and connects to patterns of human expression which are more adept at understanding our rapidly changing world.

Is McLuhan still relevant? On May 23, 2016, Pope Francis told Ahmad el-Tayeb – grand imam of al-Azhar University – that "the meeting is the message" (Esteves, 2016). Yes, indeed, and in the age of social media, such meetings can take place either in person, or any places in the world, any time, two or more people may happen to be. And in a telling synchrony between reality and televised fantasy, the fictional Pius XIII in the second episode of HBO's *The Young Pope* (HBO, 2017) insists on addressing the assembled masses in silhouetted shadow, because he knows ultimate power is conveyed by the unseen – or, as McLuhan might have put it, the supremely cool. In a related vein, David Lynch's *Twin Peaks: The Return* in 2017 continues to be most fathomable via McLuhan's notion that the electric light bulb is all medium and no message (McLuhan, 1964, p. 151; see Levinson, 2017c, for more on McLuhan and *Twin Peaks*, and also Levinson, 2017b, for an extensive, annotated bibliography of works by and about McLuhan through the present, including not only books and articles but conferences, documentaries, and other media). The same could be said of Donald Trump, whose focus, not on what he says, and whether it has any resemblance to the truth, but on saying something, anything, that attracts media interest, is a startling example of all medium and no content, or another expression of maximum fill-in-the blanks cool.

Social media themselves are unsurprisingly very aware of McLuhan's relevance to their very existence. Google devoted a Doodle to McLuhan and his work on the 106th anniversary of his birth (Google Doodle Archives, 2017, and see Levinson, 2017d).

The Google Doodle captures McLuhan's thinking about the evolution of media perfectly:

- Frame 1 shows the origin of humanity, communicating around the fire in prehistoric times, by the only medium available at that time: speech. Word of mouth was and continues to be our most fundamental mode of discourse. McLuhan referred to this as the acoustic mode.

- Frame 2 shows a civilization-making game change: writing. With the written word, ideas of any kind can be communicated without the creator of the ideas present. You can even communicate about things that have no physical existence - abstractions, such as freedom and love. Democracy, science, and of course written history all owe their origins to the written word. McLuhan called this the visual mode.

- Frame 3 shows the height of written civilization: the invention of the automobile, produced on the assembly line. In this part of our history, both speech and writing were enhanced by transportation. McLuhan looked at transportation as, in effect, another kind of communication, or an amplifier of media. In the case of the car, its interchangeable parts were the physical equivalent of the visual letters of the alphabet, and the way they can be put together to make different words.

- Frame 4 of course shows television. McLuhan correctly pointed out that although we watch television, it's actually an acoustic medium more than a visual medium. Everyone who watches the same channel on television sees the same thing at the same time, just as is the case when everyone listens to one person talking. This is unlike the written word in a book or even in a newspaper, which is read at different times by each person reading. When McLuhan said electronic media are turning the world into a global village, he was referring to everyone watching the same thing on television at the same time, just as people would who are gathered around a speaker in the village square all hear the speaker at the same time.

- And finally Frames 5 and 6 should be taken as a couplet: McLuhan's global village was not only about television but, presciently, about the Internet. The television global village was actually incomplete in two ways: It was national not global (there was no intentional television in the early 1960s when McLuhan came up with this term), and the communication was one way – unlike a village, in which everyone can be both a sender and a receiver of information, the television audience can only receive information. But the Internet has changed all of that: it was truly global, and anyone on Twitter, Facebook, YouTube, Instagram, and Snapchat can just as easily create and send content as receive it. The people at Google were keenly aware that McLuhan foresaw their very existence.

Indeed, everyone who thinks about communication – whether filmmaker, social media titan, or student – continues to apply and enact McLuhan's ideas. In my "Digital Media and Public Responsibility" class at Fordham University in May 2017, we discussed how different sports were better suited to reporting and fan involvement via different media. McLuhan (1964, p. 284) had observed more than 50 years ago that fast-moving images on television did a much better job conveying the quick game of simultaneous team action that is American football than did the slower pace of printed words in the press and radio narration, which excelled in covering pitch-by-pitch baseball (thus anticipating the 110+ million viewers of the Super Bowl, the most watched yearly event on television). Twitter, being both letters and instant, is doing well as a medium for fans of both games. I asked the class which of the two sports would work better on Snapchat. "Neither," answered one of my students, Carlo Mazzoni, who explained that the vertical orientation of photos on Snapchat would make it awkward as medium for football as well as baseball, both of which needed the wider frame of a landscape presentation.

In other words, whether 1964 or 2018, and indeed through all human history and futures, the medium is the message – and that insight applies not only to sports, but every aspect of our lives.

WHAT TO EXPECT IN THE 2020 U.S. PRESIDENTIAL ELECTION

With the increasing wisdom of hindsight, we can declare that Barack Obama concluded the age of the telegenic President that began with JFK, and continued through Ronald Reagan and Bill Clinton. In the 2009 edition of *New New Media* (p. 63), I found Paul Saffo's (2008) designation of Obama as "cybergenic" (looks good on YouTube) not entirely apt, because it "misses the crucial role that looking and sounding good on television plays in making a candidate cybergenic". In other words, Obama was not just the first Internet President – he was also the last telegenic President. In contrast, all but Donald Trump's most ardent supporters acknowledge that he does not look good on television (e.g., Nyren, 2018). But few have finished the thought with the recognition that he doesn't have to. Television is no longer the predominant political medium. Twitter is, and Trump is a master of that medium.

One response to this harsh truth has been to call for government regulation of social media like "cigarettes" or any "addictive" drug (KCBS, 2018). Not only would this be a violation of the First Amendment, and especially dangerous given Trump's antipathy to media criticism and his current residence in the White House (Levinson, 2016g), it won't work, for the same reasons Nazi Germany failed to eliminate primitive photocopying machines as disseminators of criticism of the state (Dumbach & Newborn, 1986), or the Soviet Union the "samizdat" videos which did the same in the 1980s (Levinson, 1992, pp. 195-197). Communications media have shown a stubborn resistance to government regulation and attempts to shut them down.

A better response, as indicated above, would be to field an opposing candidate who is not only telegenic – optional in our age of social media – but at least as Twittergenic or social-media-genic as Donald Trump.

Elizabeth Warren might well be such a candidate. Reports about her rally in Washington Square Park in New York City on September 16, 2019 had two significant headlines: she attracted an audience of some 20,000 people, and she devoted four hours after her speech to posing for selfies with everyone in the crowd who wanted one (Weber, 2019). Warren demonstrated that the physical crowd in politics had flipped into the selfie, and its posting on Twitter and Instagram. Her use of the inherently social two-person selfie, in addition to its offering to all who requested one, is also a democratic, communal flip of Trump's self-aggrandizing, argumentative use of Twitter. Warren acknowledged as much in the subsequent Fourth Democratic Presidential debate which took place on October 15, 2019, remarking about her abundant political selfies, perhaps with a dollop of irony, that "selfies must be the new measure of democracy".

In contrast, in that same debate, Kamala Harris showed a poor understanding of social media – or at least, their relation to the First Amendment – when she called upon Warren to join Harris in asking Twitter to ban Donald Trump's account, i.e., prevent him from tweeting. Although such an action would not explicitly violate the First Amendment, since Twitter is not a government agency, blocking the President of the United States, or any public official, from tweeting would certainly violate what I call "the spirit of the First Amendment" (Levinson, 2010), and runs contrary to the July 2019 U. S. Court of Appeals decision which held that Trump's blocking of unwelcome followers, or people critical of him, is unconstitutional, since the entire public is entitled to have access to the President's public statements (Levinson, 2019). Wisely, Harris did not accept Harris's invitation.

Meanwhile, under pressure of impeachment, Trump's increasingly volatile press conferences (e.g., Grynbaum, 2019), may indicate that he's starting to revert or flip back to the televised confrontation as his favored medium, both for the opportunity it affords to let him see the impact of his insults on the faces of the reporters he harangues in the press corps, and its visceral impact on the wider television audience.

IMPEACHMENT 2019

And Donald Trump's impeachment indeed came.

"It started with a phone call," Brian Williams aptly said on his MSNBC show, The 11th Hour (2019), about what ignited the 18 December 2019 impeachment of Donald Trump by the House of Representatives. That phone call, as everyone knows, was the one in which Trump tried to extort Volodymyr Zelensky, President of the Ukraine, to announce an investigation into Joe Biden and his son – "arms for dirt," as Former Federal Prosecutor Glenn Kirschner (2019) characterized the price (dirt on the Bidens) that Trump was attempting to exact from Zelensky for release of crucial U. S. weaponry to the Ukrainians.

But the phone call was leaky. It was overheard, and then became known to the world via a whistleblower's work. The Nixon tapes in 1974, which resulted in Nixon's resignation in order to avoid impeachment, became the phone call in 2019 which made Trump's impeachment unavoidable unless he too had resigned, which he did not.

And in the aftermath of that phone call, television took front and center stage, including through the vote for impeachment. Traditional media, telephone and television, brought a President to the edge of removal, just as the tapes had done to Nixon.

It is significant that, with all the attention Twitter and social media correctly receive as vehicles and conduits of politics today, it was two traditional media that carried the ball for impeachment in the age of Trump. Which is evidence of a point I often make, highly consistent with McLuhan's tetrad and his study of older vs. newer media: new media rarely obliterate older media. Instead, though the newer media get most of the attention, the older media continue to do their job.

Tape recording, telephone, television. Older media, with venerable values. Much like democracy itself.

Stay tuned.

--Paul Levinson, December 2019, New York City (first published October 2015)

BIBLIOGRAPHY

Andrews, Natalie (2016) "Hillary Clinton's Campaign Uses Pokémon Go to Register Voters," *The Wall Street Journal,* 16 July. http://blogs.wsj.com/washwire/2016/07/16/hillary-clintons-campaign-uses-pokemon-go-to-register-voters/

Asimov, Isaac (1974) *The Foundation Trilogy.* New York: Avon. First published as a series of short stories in the 1940s, and then as three novels in the 1950s.

Bailey, Jason (2016) "Everything is Fine: House Republicans Propose Fines for Congressional Live-Streams," *Flavorwire,* 27 December.
http://flavorwire.com/596437/everything-is-fine-house-republicans-propose-fines-for-congressional-live-streams

Bazin, André (1962/1967) *Qu'est-ce que le cinema?* Trans. Hugh Gray, *What Is Cinema?* Berkelely: CA: University of California Press.

Brzeski, Patrick (2019) "Universal's Beijing Theme Park Adds Alibaba as Strategic Partner," *The Hollywood Reporter,* 16 October. https://www.hollywoodreporter.com/news/universals-beijing-theme-park-adds-alibaba-as-partner-1248421

Campbell, Andy (2016) "Brendan Dassey's Conviction Overturned After 'Making A Murderer' Tells His Story," The Huffington Post, 12 August.
http://www.huffingtonpost.com/entry/brendan-dasseys-conviction-overturned-making-a-mur-

derer_us_57ae2f42e4b0718404117823

CBS News (2016) "Is Trump 'Softening' or 'Hardening' on Immigration?" 29 August.
http://www.cbsnews.com/videos/is-trump-softening-or-hardening-on-immigration/

Clinton, Hillary (1996) *It Takes A Village*. New York: Simon & Schuster.

CNN (2017) "Donald Trump shuts down CNN reporter: "You're fake news," 11 January. Video: https://youtu.be/Vqpzk-qGxMU

Corasaniti, Nick (2015) "Donald Trump Releases Plan to Combat Illegal Immigration," *The New York Times*, 16 August. http://www.nytimes.com/2015/08/17/us/politics/trump-releases-plan-to-combat-illegal-immigration.html

Davis, Wynne (2016) "Fake or Real?" *All Tech Considered*, NPR, 5 December.
http://www.npr.org/sections/alltechconsidered/2016/12/05/503581220/fake-or-real-how-to-self-check-the-news-and-get-the-facts

Dugyala, Rishika (2019) “House members debate possible ‘witness intimidation’ by Trump,“ *Politico*, 17 November. https://www.politico.com/news/2019/11/17/trump-tweets-witness-intimidation-stewart-maloney-071308

Dumbach, Annette E. & Newborn, Jud (1986) *Shattering the German Night: The Story of the White Rose.* New York: Little, Brown.

Easley, Jonathan (2016) "WHIP LIST: Republicans breaking with Trump," *The Hill*, 8 October.
http://thehill.com/homenews/campaign/300011-whip-list-republicans-breaking-with-trump

Eller, Nikki (2016) "Playing for Change: Making peace through music," *Humanosphere*, 22 July. http://www.humanosphere.org/basics/2016/07/playing-change-making-peace-music/

Esteves, Junno Arocho (2016) "'The meeting is the message,' Pope tells head of al-Azhar," *National Catholic Reporter*, 23 May. http://ncronline.org/news/vatican/meeting-message-pope-tells-head-al-azhar

Evangelista, Benny (2011) "Facebook, Twitter and Egypt's upheaval," SF Gate, 13 February. http://www.sfgate.com/cgibin/article.cgi?f=/c/a/2011/02/12/BUGN1HLHTR.DTL

Fineman, Howard (2016) comments on *MSNBC-Live with Tamron Hall*, MSNBC-TV, 3 August.

Flood, Alison (2015) "Japanese Bookshop Stocks Only One Book at a Time, *The Guardian*, 23 December. http://www.theguardian.com/books/2015/dec/23/japanese-bookshop-stocks-only-one-book-at-a-time

Friedersdorf, Connor (2016) "Donald Trump's Most Politically Correct Speech (Aided by a TelePrompter)," *The Atlantic*, 7 June. http://www.theatlantic.com/politics/archive/2016/06/donald-trumps-politically-correct-speech-aided-by-a-tele-prompter/486134/

Gass, Nick (2016) "Clinton: 'I am not a natural politician'," *Politico*, 9 March. http://www.politico.com/blogs/2016-dem-primary-live-updates-and-results/2016/03/hillary-clinton-i-am-not-a-natural-politician-220544

Google Doodle Archives (2017) "Marshall McLuhan's 106th Birthday," 21 July. https://www.google.com/doodles/marshall-mcluhans-106th-birthday

Gray, Thomas (1751) "Elegy Written in a Country Churchyard," poem.

Grynbaum, Michael M. (2019) “Reporter’s Question, Repeated, Sets Trump on Latest Media Attack,” *The New York Times*, 2 October. https://www.nytimes.com/2019/10/02/business/media/trump-media-attack.html

Harding, Xavier (2016) "The Snapchat Spectacles craze, explained," *Vox*, 14 December.
http://www.vox.com/new-money/2016/12/14/13945736/snapchat-spectacles-craze-explained

Hardwick, Chris (2015) *The Talking Dead*, AMC-TV, 22 November.

HBO (2017) *The Young Pope*, created and directed by Paolo Sorrentino, episode 2, 16 January.

Healy, Patrick; Parker, Ashley; Haberman, Maggie (2016) "New Debate Strategy for Donald Trump: Practice, Practice, Practice," *The New York Times*, 28 September.
http://www.nytimes.com/2016/09/29/us/politics/donald-trump-debate.html

Hill, Libby (2017) "The Beatles coming to SiriusXM, 24 hours a day, 8 days a week," *Los Angeles Times*, 2 May. http://www.latimes.com/entertainment/la-et-entertainment-news-updates-may-the-beatles-coming-to-siriusxm-24-1493752738-htmlstory.html

Hitler, Adolf (1924/1971) *Mein Kampf*, trans. R. Manheim, Boston: Houghton-Mifflin.

Howey, Hugh C. (2016) "Rock, Paper, Scissors," *The Wayfinder*, 10 September.
http://www.hughhowey.com/rock-paper-scissors/

Hunt, Arthur W., III (2016) "Donald Trump: Hot Persona for a Cool Medium," *Second Nature*, 25 January.
http://secondnaturejournal.com/donald-trump-hot-persona-for-a-cool-medium/

Kastrenakes, Jacob (2016) "C-SPAN is using Periscope and Facebook Live to Broadcast the House Sit-In," *The Verge*, 22 June. http://www.theverge.com/2016/6/22/12006500/c-span-uses-periscope-facebook-live-for-house-protest

Kaufman, Sarah L. (2015) "Why Obama's singing of 'Amazing Grace' is so powerful," *Washington Post*, 26 June. https://www.washingtonpost.com/news/arts-and-entertainment/wp/2015/06/26/why-obamas-singing-of-amazing-grace-is-so-powerful

KCBS (2018) "Salesforce CEO Benioff Compares Facebook To 'Big Tobacco'," 23 January. http://sanfrancisco.cbslocal.com/2018/01/23/salesforce-ceo-benioff-compares-facebook-big-tobacco/

Kirschner, Glenn (2019) "Hardball," MSNBC, 13 November.

Kornfeld, Leora (2016) "*McLuhan in an Age of Social Media*: Tweets from a Book Salon I Could Not Attend," *De-Mass'd* blog, 27 January. http://demassed.blogspot.com/2016/01/quick-posttonight-as-tomorrow-is.html

Lawson, Victoria C. (2018) "Smartphone keys– killing or capitalising guest experience?" *Medium*, 30 January. https://medium.com/the-hotels-network/smartphones-keys-killing-or-capitalising-guest-experience-dbbfcbf137d6

Levinson, Paul (1976) "'Hot' and 'Cool' Redefined for Interactive Media," *Media Ecology Review*, *4 (3)*, pp. 9-11.

______ (1979) "Human Replay: A Theory of the Evolution of Media," PhD dissertation, New York University. (Now available in Kindle and paperback.)

_____ (1992) *Electronic Chronicles: Columns of the Changes in our Time*. San Francisco, CA: Anamnesis Press.

______(1996a) "The Shorter Foundation of Science Fiction," *Journal of Social and Evolutionary Systems, 19/3*, pp. 207-215. https://www.academia.edu/27383059/The_shorter_foundation_of_science_fiction

_____ (1996b) "On Behalf of Humanity: The Technological Edge," *The World and I*, March. https://www.worldandischool.com/public/1996/March/school-resource15056.asp

______(1997) *The Soft Edge: A Natural History and Future of the Information Revolution.* London & New York: Routledge.

______(1999) *Digital McLuhan: A Guide to the Information Millennium.* London & New York: Routledge.

______(2003) *Realspace: The Fate of Physical Presence in the Digital Age, On and Off Planet.* London & New York: Routledge.

_____ (2007a) "The Sopranos End and the Closure-Junkies," *Infinite Regress* blog, 12 June. http://paullevinson.blogspot.com/2007/06/sopranos-end-and-closure-junkies.html Expanded and reprinted as "The Sopranos and the Closure Junkies" in *The Essential Sopranos Reader*, eds. David Lavery, Douglas Howard, and Paul Levinson. Lexington, KY: University Press of Kentucky, 2011, pp. 313-316.

_____(2007b) "Battle of Videos: Hillary Clinton and The Sopranos! v. Obama Girl," *Infinite Regress* blog, 19 June. http://paullevinson.blogspot.com/2007/06/hillary-clinton-and-sopranos.html

_____(2007c) "*Mad Men* 6: The Medium is the Message!" *Infinite Regress* blog, 24 August. http://paullevinson.blogspot.com/2007/08/mad-men-6-medium-is-message.html

_____ (2009/2013) *New New Media.* New York: Pearson.

_____ (2010) "Blagojevich and Fair Trial 1, Fitzgerald 0," Infinite Regress blog, 10 April. http://paullevinson.blogspot.com/2010/08/blagojevich-and-fair-trial-1-fitzgerald.html

_____ (2011) “Marshall McLuhan, North Africa, and social media,” lecture at
St. Francis College, Brooklyn, NY, 23 February.
video: http://youtu.be/FVX5m7P0Zsg

_____ (2014) "The Kindle Arrives in Time and Makes Everyone a Publisher," *Journal of Visual Culture, 13/1*, 70-72.

_____ (2015a) "Excellent, McLuhanesque Hillary Clinton Announcement Video," *Infinite Regress* blog, 12 April. http://paullevinson.blogspot.com/2015/04/excellent-mcluhanesque-hillary-clinton.html

_____(2015b) "The End of an Era and the Ultimate Cool," *Infinite Regress* blog, 18 May. http://paullevinson.blogspot.com/2015/05/mad-men-end-of-era-and-ultimate-cool.html

_____(2015c) Interview by Mike Hosking, *Breakfast* Radio, New Zealand, 6 December.

_____(2016a) "*Making a Murderer*: Showing Us the Truth about our Unjust Justice System," *Infinite Regress* blog, 7 January. http://paullevinson.blogspot.com/2016/01/making-murderer-showing-us-truth-about.html

_____(2016b) Interview by Zach Atanasoff, *Issues Tank*, WFUV-FM Radio, 30 June.
http://www.wfuv.org/content/issues-tank-new-gen-block

_____(2016c) Interview by Joe Concha, "Trump-Clinton debate expected to shatter records," *The Hill*, 20 September.
http://thehill.com/homenews/administration/296818-trump-clinton-debate-expected-to-shatter-ratings-records

_____(2016d) "Marshall McLuhan, Donald Trump, and the Revenge Cool." Paper presented at the Toronto School: Then, Now,

Next conference, 14 October.

_____(2016e) Interview by Amanda Hoover, "How curated articles could help Facebook fight fake news," *Christian Science Monitor*, 4 December. http://www.csmonitor.com/Technology/2016/1204/How-curated-articles-could-help-Facebook-fight-fake-news

_____(2016f) "McLuhan, Trump, and the Problem of Fake News." Lecture via Skype at Faculty of Journalism, Information, and Book Studies, University of Warsaw, Poland, 8 December. video: https://youtu.be/lefQsM8xDss

_____(2016g) *Fake News in Real Context.* New York: Connected Editions.

_____ (2017a) "*The Perversity of Things*: review #3 of X: The Evolution of Media," *Infinite Regress* blog, 2 January. http://paullevinson.blogspot.com/2017/01/the-perversity-of-things-review-3-of-x.html

_____ (2017b) "Marshall McLuhan," *Oxford Bibliographies in Communication*, ed. Patricia Moy, New York: Oxford University Press. http://www.oxfordbibliographies.com/view/document/obo-9780199756841/obo-9780199756841-0139.xml

_____ (2017c) "Review of *Twin Peaks: The Return* 1.5: *The Mod Squad* Meets *Big Love* in the Diner," *Omni*, 5 June. https://omni.media/review-of-twin-peaks-the-return-1-5

_____ (2017d) "A Marshall McLuhan expert annotates the Google Doodle honoring the Internet visionary," with Introduction by Kira Bindrim, *Quartz*, 21 July. https://qz.com/1035889/a-marshall-mcluhan-expert-annotates-the-google-doodle-honoring-the-internet-visionary/

_____ (2019) "Prohibiting Presidential Blocking of Twitter Critics Is Good for Democracy," *The Globe Post*, 17 July. https://theglobepost.com/2019/07/17/trump-twitter-democracy/

McCartney, Paul (1973) "Let Me Roll It," 1st recorded by Paul McCartney and Wings on 1973 LP, *Band on the Run*, Apple Records.

McDermott, Maeve (2018) "Late night burns Trump for firing 'human Grumpy Cat' Rex Tillerson via tweet," *USA Today*, 14 March. https://www.usatoday.com/story/life/entertainthis/2018/03/14/late-night-ethers-trump-firing-human-grumpy-cat-rex-tillerson-via-tweet/423259002/

McLuhan, Marshall (1951) *The Mechanical Bride*, New York: Vanguard.

_____ (1960) "Report on Project in Understanding New Media," National Association of Educational Broadcasters, U. S. Department of Health, Education, and Welfare, 30 June.

_____ (1962) *The Gutenberg Galaxy*. New York: Mentor.

_____ (1964) *Understanding Media*, 2nd ed. New York: Mentor.

_____ (1972) *Take Today: The Executive as Dropout*. New York: Harcourt Brace Jovanovich.

_____ (1977) "The Laws of the Media," Preface by Paul Levinson, *et cetera (34) 2*, pp. 173–179.

_____(1978) "A Last Look at the Tube," *New York Magazine*, 3 April, p. 45.

_____ (2019) "Prohibiting Presidential Blocking of Twitter Critics Is Good for Democracy," The Globe Post, 17 July. https://theglobepost.com/2019/07/17/trump-twitter-democracy/

Moreno, Jonathan D. (2016) "GOP - Bioethics = Trump," *HuffPost*

Politics, 19 March. http://www.huffingtonpost.com/jonathan-d-moreno/gop---bioethics--trump_b_9507916.html

Morning Joe (2016) "Donald Trump Won't Pursue Hillary Clinton Investigations," MSNBC, 22 November. https://www.youtube.com/watch?v=nnefuPa7EEE

New York Times, The (2015) "End the Gun Epidemic in America," Editorial, 5 December, p. 1.

Nyren, Erin (2018) "Late Night Hosts Mock Trump for Botching National Anthem," *Variety*, 9 January. http://variety.com/2018/tv/news/late-night-trump-national-anthem-1202659466/

O'Donnell, Lawrence (2015) *The Last Word*, MSNBC-TV, 22 October.

Pew Research Center (2015) "Most Millennials Resist the 'Millennial' Label," 3 September. http://www.people-press.org/2015/09/03/most-millennials-resist-the-millennial-label/

Phippen, Thomas (2017) "Trump Says His Twitter Account Will Continue To Get Around The 'Dishonest' Press," *The Daily Caller*, January 16. http://dailycaller.com/2017/01/16/trump-says-his-twitter-account-will-continue-to-get-around-the-dishonest-press/

Pooley, Jefferson (2016) "How to Become a Famous Media Scholar: The Case of Marshall McLuhan," *Los Angeles Review of Books*, 20 December. https://lareviewofbooks.org/article/become-famous-media-scholar-case-marshall-mcluhan

Postman, Andrew (2017) "My dad predicted Trump in

1985 – it's not Orwell, he warned, it's Brave New World," *The Guardian*, 2 February. https://www.theguardian.com/media/2017/feb/02/amusing-ourselves-to-death-neil-postman-trump-orwell-huxley

"Proverb: It Takes a Whole Village to Raise a Child" (1996), *HNet*, 25 January. http://www.h-net.org/~africa/threads/village.html

Robinson, Eugene (2016) Coverage of 2016 Republican National Convention, MSNBC-TV, 18 July.

Saffo, Paul (2008) "Obama's 'Cybergenic' Edge," abcnews.com, 11 June. http://abcnews.go.com/Technology/Politics/Story?id=5046275

Savage, Charlie (2017) "Twitter Users Blocked by Trump File Lawsuit," *The New York Times*, 11 July. https://www.nytimes.com/2017/07/11/us/politics/trump-twitter-users-lawsuit.html

Savransky, Rebecca (2017) "Trump: Whether it's a ban or not, it's keeping 'bad people' out," *The Hill*, 1 February. http://thehill.com/homenews/administration/317279-trump-call-immigration-order-what-you-want

Schwartz, Tony (1973) *The Responsive Chord.* New York: Anchor/Doubleday. (Second edition, with Foreword by John Carey, Coral Gables, FL: Mango, 2017)

Sheehy, Gail (1999) *Hillary's Choice.* New York: Random House.

Silver, Nate (2016) "Election Update: Polls Show Potential Fallout From Trump Tape," *FiveThirtyEight*, 10 October. http://fivethirtyeight.com/features/election-update-polls-show-potential-fallout-from-trump-tape/

Slater, Robert (2007) *No Such Thing as Over-Exposure: Inside the Life and Celebrity of Donald Trump.* New York: Prentice Hall.

Stelter, Brian (2016) "Debate breaks record as most-watched in U.S. history," *CNN Money*, 27 September.
http://money.cnn.com/2016/09/27/media/debate-ratings-record-viewership/

Strate, Lance (2004) "Ong Presides," *Explorations in Media Ecology, (3) 1*, pp. 65-66.

Straczynski, J. Michael; Wachowski, Lana; Wachowski, Lily (2016) *Sense8*, Netflix, Christmas special.

Streitfeld, David (2017) "'The Internet Is Broken': @ev Is Trying to Salvage It," *The New York Times,* 20 May. https://www.nytimes.com/2017/05/20/technology/evan-williams-medium-twitter-internet.html

Sturt, David & Nordstrom, Todd (2016) " What Pokémon Go Might Say About Mankind, And Your Success At Work," *Forbes,* 16 July. http://www.forbes.com/sites/davidsturt/2016/07/16/what-pokemon-go-might-say-about-mankind-and-your-success-at-work/#c9272bf6a271

Toole, John Kennedy (1980) *A Confederacy of Dunces*. Baton Rouge, LA: Louisiana State University Press.

Trump, Donald T. (2015) "I'm not a politician ...," 11 August.
http://www.cnn.com/videos/tv/2015/08/11/donald-trump-part-five-interview-newday.cnn

Van Susteren, Greta (2016) "Who's To Blame for Fake News," *Los Angeles Times*, 5 December.
http://www.latimes.com/opinion/op-ed/la-oe-van-susteren-fake-news-20161205-story.html

Warren, Elizabeth (2019) Fourth Democratic Presidential Debate, CNN, 15 October.

WashPostPR (2017) "*The Washington Post* will be the breaking news source on Snapchat's Discover," *Wash-*

ington Post, 13 February. https://www.washington-post.com/pr/wp/2017/02/13/the-washington-post-will-be-the-breaking-news-source-on-snapchats-discover

Weber, Peter (2019) "Elizabeth Warren capped her big anti-corruption speech in New York with 4 hours of selfies," The Week, 17 September. https://theweek.com/speedreads/865378/elizabeth-warren-capped-big-anticorruption-speech-new-york-4-hours-selfies

Williams, Brian (2019) "The 11th Hour," MSNBC, 18 December.

Wythoff, Grant, ed. (2016) *The Perversity of Things: Hugo Gernsback on Media, Tinkering, and Scientifiction.* Minneapolis, MN: University of Minnesota Press.

VIDEOS BY PAUL LEVINSON ABOUT MARSHALL MCLUHAN

(2011) "Marshall McLuhan, North Africa, and Social Media," lecture at St. Francis College, Brooklyn, NY, 23 February, https://youtu.be/FVX5m7P0Zsg

(2012) "Marshall McLuhan: Then and Now," interview from J. Charles Sterin's multi-media book, *Mass Media Revolution*, https://youtu.be/L3V_p8YDboE

(2013) "Transmedia Transnational Video Journalism," TEDx talk at St. Peter's University, Jersey City, NJ, 21 March, https://youtu.be/f3F7vp99o7Y

(2014) "The Medium of the Book, 50 Years after *Understanding Media*," Keynote Address at Baylor Libraries 2014 Symposium, *50 Years after McLuhan*,
Baylor University, Waco, TX, 25 September, https://youtu.be/somk7CpeOcI

(2016) "Marshall McLuhan, Donald Trump, and the Revenge of Cool," lecture at the Players Club in New York City for the New York Society of General Semantics, 9 September, https://youtu.be/RhWrN1zdHps

(2016) "McLuhan, Trump, and the Problem of Fake News," lecture via Skype at Faculty of Journalism, Information, and Book Studies, University of Warsaw, Poland, 8 December, https://youtu.be/lefQsM8xDss

(2017) "McLuhan in New York," Eric McLuhan, Paul Levinson, John Carey deliver lectures on the 50th anniversary of McLuhan's 1967-1968 year at Fordham University (October 13, 2017 lectures at Fordham University, Lincoln Center, New York City) https://youtu.be/QK8A2PQux3I

(2017) "The Omnipotent Ear," lecture about the "flip" of binge-watching television into binge-listening to the Beatles on Sirius XM Radio, delivered at McLuhan in New York event, 13 October, https://youtu.be/Hb7pk3OSN1k

(2019) "How I Met Marshall McLuhan," Liquid Lunch, ThatChannel.com, 11min 50 sec into interview, 20 November. https://youtu.be/5jUzIcxNwW0

ABOUT THE AUTHOR

Paul Levinson, PhD, is Professor of Communication & Media Studies at Fordham University in NYC. His nonfiction books, including *The Soft Edge* (1997), *Digital McLuhan* (1999), *Realspace* (2003), *Cellphone* (2004), and *New New Media* (2009; 2nd edition, 2012), have been translated into fifteen languages. His science fiction novels include *The Silk Code* (winner of Locus Award for Best First Science Fiction Novel of 1999), *Borrowed Tides* (2001), *The Consciousness Plague* (2002), *The Pixel Eye* (2003), *The Plot To Save Socrates* (2006), *Unburning Alexandria* (2013), and *Chronica* (2014) - the last three of which are also known as the Sierra Waters trilogy, and are historical as well as science fiction. His novelette, "The Chronology Protection Case," was made into a short movie available on Amazon Prime. He appears on CNN, MSNBC, Fox News, the Discovery Channel, National Geographic, the History Channel, NPR, and numerous TV and radio programs. His 1972 LP, *Twice Upon a Rhyme*, was re-issued in 2010. He reviews television in his InfiniteRegress.tv blog, and was listed in *The Chronicle of Higher Education*'s "Top 10 Academic Twitterers" in 2009.

The following books by Paul Levinson are available on Kindle and paperback:

Nonfiction:

The Soft Edge: A Natural History and Future of the Information Revolution

Digital McLuhan: A Guide to the Information Millennium

Realspace: The Fate of Physical Presence in the Digital Age, On and Off Planet

New New Media

From Media Theory to Space Odyssey: Petar Jandrić interviews Paul Levinson

Fake News in Real Context

Cyber War and Peace

Human Replay: A Theory of the Evolution of Media, original PhD dissertation, 1979, New York University.

Science fiction:

Loose Ends (time travel) series (complete):
Loose Ends, Little Differences, Late Lessons, Last Calls

Sierra Waters (time travel) series:
The Plot to Save Socrates, Unburning Alexandria, Chronica

Phil D'Amato forensic detective series:
The Chronology Protection Case, The Silk Code, The Consciousness Plague, The Pixel Eye

Ian's Ions and Eons (three time travel novelettes)

Exo-Genetic Engineers series
The Orchard, The Suspended Fourth

Double Realities series
The Other Car, Extra Credit, The Wallet

Borrowed Tides

Marilyn and Monet

The Kid in the Video Store

Peter Brown Called: Tales of SciFi and Music

Urban Corridors: Fables and Gables

Robinson Calculator

Nonfiction and Science Fiction

Touching the Face of the Cosmos: On the Intersection of Space Travel and Religion
an anthology of essays and science fiction stories, including a new interview with John Glenn, an essay by Guy Consolmagno, SJ (the "Pope's Astronomer"), and contributions from leading thinkers about the role of religion in space travel

Interested in occasional announcements about my books?
Follow me on Twitter @PaulLev or sign up for my mailing list.

Paul Levinson

Fake News in Real Context

Made in the USA
Middletown, DE
11 January 2020